LINDA BOZZO

AMAZING ANIMAL SKIN

PowerKiDS press

New York

To my family and friends and all of your amazing features that make you who you are.
—LBS

Published in 2008 by The Rosen Publishing Group, Inc.
29 East 21st Street, New York, NY 10010

First Edition

Editor: Joanne Randolph
Book Design: Kate Laczynski
Photo Researcher: Nicole Pristash

Photo Credits: Cover © Morales/agefotostock.com; pp. 5, 7, 9, 11, 13, 15, 19, 21 Shutterstock.com; p. 17 © Greg Brzezinski/www.istockphoto.com.

Library of Congress Cataloging-in-Publication Data

Bozzo, Linda.
   Amazing animal skin / Linda Bozzo. — 1st ed.
      p. cm. — (Creature features)
   Includes index.
   ISBN 978-1-4042-4168-8 (library binding)
   1. Skin—Juvenile literature. 2. Hair—Juvenile literature. I. Title.
   QL941.B69 2008
   591.47—dc22
                                        2007025881

Manufactured in the United States of America

CONTENTS

SKIN DEEP

Animals have many different types of skin, or hide. An animal's hide can help it stay safe in its **habitat**. A snake has special skin made up of tiny plates, called scales. The pointy porcupine has hair that can go on the **attack**.

Many of these animals' hides have **adapted** over time to their habitat. Some animals live in the cold where having a furry coat comes in handy. Other animals have skin that lets them live in the rain forest or by a pond. Animals live in many different places, and they have skin that makes them suited to their home.

The skin of a poison dart frog, like this one, can kill the unlucky animal that tries to eat the frog.

SHEDDING SNAKES

There are about 2,700 kinds of snakes in the world. All of them have skin made of scales. A snake's scales allow it to move and bend freely.

A snake's smooth, dry skin has colors and markings on it that help it hide. This keeps the snake safe and helps it hunt for **prey**.

When a snake grows, its skin does not. It needs to shed its old skin by crawling out of it. A new skin is ready to take the place of the old one.

You can see the small overlapping scales that make up this snake's skin. A snake has no legs, so it uses the scales on its underside to pull itself along the ground.

REAL-LIFE DRAGONS!

Dragons are just make-believe, right? Tell that to the sea dragons swimming in the warm ocean waters of Australia!

There are two kinds of sea dragons. There are leafy sea dragons and weedy sea dragons. These fish call beds of seaweed and sea grass home. Sea dragons' skin makes them look just like the plants in their habitat. They have many parts sticking out from their skin. These leaflike pieces **camouflage** sea dragons and keep them safe from other fish. Sea dragons truly have some amazing skin!

This leafy sea dragon has green parts coming out of its yellow body. These green pieces look just like the seaweed in which the leafy sea dragon makes its home.

THE MUDDY RHINOCEROS

What animal has a horn on its nose, has thick, gray skin, and eats only plants? If you said a rhinoceros, you are right! Rhinos love to roll around in the mud. This is called wallowing. Covering the rhino's skin with mud helps to keep this large animal cool. It also stops bugs from biting.

A rhinoceros has **tough** skin to keep it safe. Its skin is nearly ½ inch (1 cm) thick. That is pretty thick for skin! Rhinos like to get into fights, so this tough, thick skin really comes in handy.

Did you know that the rhino's horn is made out of the same stuff our hair and fingernails are made of? The horn is still very strong and keeps the rhino safe.

POLAR-BEAR HAIR

Imagine living someplace where it is so cold there is always ice on the ground. Polar bears live in just such a place. They live in the icy, snowy Arctic. Polar bears can live here because of their fur and skin.

A polar bear's fur looks white, but it is made up of lots of clear, **hollow** hairs. The sun goes right through these hairs to the bear's black skin. Things that are black **absorb** light and heat. This helps warm the bear's body in the cold. The hairs also keep the bear's body heat from leaving.

The polar bear's clear hairs also help the bear float when it swims. There is even thick hair on a polar bear's feet to keep it from falling on the ice.

THE OKAPI'S UMBRELLA

Did you see something move over there? It takes luck and good eyesight to spot the okapi. Its skin helps it blend in with the trees. Some people might think the okapi looks like a zebra because it has striped legs. Okapis are really in the same family as giraffes, though.

The okapi's stripes help the animal hide from **predators**. The stripes may also help young okapis follow their mothers through the forest. The okapi's fur is also oily. This makes the rain slide off to keep the okapi dry, like an umbrella keeps you dry!

Here you can see the beautiful markings on the okapi's legs. The okapi is only found in Africa's Ituri Rain Forest.

ARMADILLO ARMOR

When most people think of an armadillo, they think of its hard shell. This shell, or **armor**, is made of bone. The armadillo may wear armor, but it is not looking for a fight. It just wants to stay safe!

When crossing streams, its heavy shell causes the armadillo to sink. It will walk along the stream bottom, where enemies cannot see it. This is one way it can use its shell to escape. Another way is to run from danger and take cover in bushes covered with **thorns**. The thorns will not hurt the hard shell of the armadillo.

This is a six-banded armadillo. This hairy armadillo gets it name because it usually has about six moveable bands of armor to help it get around.

POINTY PORCUPINE

You may have heard about a porcupine's pointy **quills**. Did you know that a porcupine has three different kinds of hair, though? One kind keeps it warm in cold weather. Another kind keeps it dry. The third kind, the quills, keeps the porcupine safe.

If an animal tries to attack, the porcupine raises its quills. It will then stick the animal with these sharp, needlelike hairs. This is very painful to its attacker. A porcupine's quills come off easily. This is so they will fall out and stay in the attacker. Like hair, porcupine quills will grow back.

The tree porcupine lives throughout South America. This porcupine's body is covered with thick, short quills that are white or yellow and dark hair that keeps it warm and dry.

IT'S ALL IN THE HAIR

Imagine taking a nap in the bathtub! The sea otter spends most of its time swimming, diving, and, yes, even sleeping in the water. It lives in the cold ocean waters near places like Alaska, Japan, and California.

The sea otter has no fat to keep it warm in its chilly home, but do not worry! The sea otter has the thickest fur of all **mammals**. The otter spends a lot of time combing its fur. This spreads oils on the fur to keep it dry and puts air bubbles between the hairs to keep the otter warm.

The sea otter has pockets of skin by its front paws. It can use these pockets to store food while it is on a dive.

THE SKIN WE'RE IN

Animals come from all parts of the world, and they live in very different habitats. This is why all animals do not look the same. Each animal's hide has adapted to work best where it lives.

There are animals with long hair. There are animals with short hair. Some animals have dry skin. Some have tough skin. These are just a few ways animals are different. No matter what type of covering animals have, they are all a part of nature. Enjoy them. They are all amazing in their own special way!

absorb (ub-SORB) To take in and hold on to something.

adapted (uh-DAPT-ed) Changed to fit requirements.

armor (AR-mer) A hard cover over something that keeps it safe.

attack (uh-TAK) An act of trying to hurt someone or something.

camouflage (KA-muh-flahj) To hide by looking like the things around one.

habitat (HA-beh-tat) The kind of land where an animal or a plant naturally lives.

hollow (HOL-oh) Having a hole through the center.

mammals (MA-mulz) Warm-blooded animals that have a backbone and hair, breathe air, and feed milk to their young.

predators (PREH-duh-terz) Animals that kill other animals for food.

prey (PRAY) An animal that is hunted by another animal for food.

quills (KWILZ) The long, sharp, thin hairs on a porcupine.

thorns (THORNZ) Sharp points on a plant.

tough (TUF) Strong or firm.

INDEX

C
coat, 4

F
fur, 12, 14, 20

H
habitat(s), 4, 8, 22
hair(s), 4, 12, 18, 20, 22

hide(s), 4, 22
home, 4, 8

M
mammals, 20

P
plates, 4
predators, 14
prey, 6

Q
quills, 18

S
scales, 4, 6
snake(s), 4, 6

W
world, 6, 22

WEB SITES

Due to the changing nature of Internet links, PowerKids Press has developed an online list of Web sites related to the subject of this book. This site is updated regularly. Please use this link to access the list:

www.powerkidslinks.com/cfeat/skin/